As I Wa

I desire to be open
To my own heart,
To others,
And to God

I desire to be responsive
To invitations to grow,
To be present,
And to rest

I desire to be intentional
In my interactions,
In acts of kindness,
And with my words

I desire to be authentic
In my humility,
In my generosity,
And in my gratitude

I desire to be free
To know, and be known,
To forgive, and be forgiven
And to love, and be loved

Amen.

The Ascent to Santiago

A Contemplative Journal
For Those
Walking the Way of St. James

RONALD K. OTTENAD

The Ascent to Santiago

Copyright © 2016 by Ronald K. Ottenad

ISBN 978-0-9864325-2-1

Printed in the United States of America

First Printing, 2016

To my wife Tammie.
There is no one with whom
I would rather walk through life.

TABLE OF CONTENTS

INTRODUCTION

Three times a year the Jewish people would set out on pilgrimage towards Jerusalem. As they made their way to the city, which is set high on a hill, they would sing the Psalms of Ascent (Psalms 120-134). These pilgrim's songs helped to prepare their hearts and souls for their arrival in Jerusalem and participation in the sacred ceremonies and celebrations. The Psalms helped these pilgrims remember who they were, reminded them of their purpose and of the strength available through God. They spoke of sorrow, distress, mercy, surrender, sovereignty, blessing, joy, unity and fellowship. These Psalms encouraged them to contemplate the reality of their hearts and how the journey was shaping them. These are powerful songs.

This journal endeavors to create the same space in your heart as you make your way towards Santiago. While the daily prompts may not be singable, they can help you remember who you are and explore what you are created to do. They will lead you to meditate on many of the themes found in the Psalms of Ascent and other truths which will become very present to you as you make your way along the Camino. They will help you to be attentive to how this journey is shaping your heart, and intentional in the contemplation of how it will inform your life after you leave Santiago.

The journal keeps pace with John Brierley's guide book, *A Pilgrim's Guide to the Camino de Santiago*, but it is not meant to be rigid. If you desire to keep tempo with the guide book, this will follow right along, but if you want to set your own timeline, the journal allows you that flexibility.

While it may not be immediately apparent, much thought has been put into the placement of each topic of contemplation. I hope this journal will act as an invitation to perceive how the physical experience of the Camino enables you to more fully discern the internal journey of your heart. The desire is for you to find yourself walking in the middle of the day and suddenly realizing how what you are experiencing in the moment is bringing meaning to what you have been contemplating. In these moments there is a synergy which gives birth to wisdom and insight. Much is discovered in the practice of walking.

Having said all that, you may find yourself drawn to a particular theme on a certain day. Feel the freedom to take the contemplative prompts in any order you wish. I only recommend you find a way of marking the order in which you travel through them, so that in the future when you return to this journal you can retrace the internal steps of your journey.

How to use this Journal

Contemplation - I would suggest you take just a few minutes before you set out in the morning to read through the day's prompt. It will not take long, and it will allow you to make the most of the quiet space mornings along the Camino provide.

It might be helpful to pull out your journal once during the day, maybe when you stop to rest or just before you set out again after lunch and reread the prompt. This will help you to refocus your heart and mind.

Journaling - After you have arrived at your destination for the day, and have settled in, find some space to put on paper what you have been turning over in your mind. The journal questions, though simple, are designed to open your heart to your experience of the internal, external and sacred worlds. At the end of the Camino, the rhythm of pausing daily to be present to your experience of each of these worlds will provide a picture of how your capacity to see them has grown.

Most of the space provided is there to allow you to freely express what you are experiencing, thinking, feeling and perceiving. There is no right way to do this. You may write in prose, create poetry, or sketch. Use the medium of expression which best captures what is going on in your mind, heart, and soul.

Writing with your opposite hand engages a different part of your brain. You may want to try this technique when you find yourself struggling to articulate what is going on internally, or when you are processing something that is rooted deeply in your past. While your penmanship may be messy, you may be surprised by the clarity this practice can bring to your thoughts. Be adventurous, try it at least once.

Meditation - In the appendix of this journal you will find passages of scripture which are excellent companions to the daily contemplative prompts. You may wish to devote a few minutes each day to reading and meditating on one.

I would suggest slowly reading through one of the short passages several times. As you do, identify a word or phrase which whispers to your heart, "Pay attention to me today." Let this be an invitation to allow these words to penetrate deeper into your soul. Permit the word or phrase to interact with those things which your heart is concerned about, longs to embrace or struggles to believe. Be open to what these words have to speak to your soul. Allow this internal dialogue to lead you to converse with

God about what is coming up in your heart. Complete your time of meditation with a few moments of silence where you simply rest in God's love and acceptance.

Finally, I want to encourage you to be expectant for what your journey will hold. Your decision to make space for the pilgrimage to Santiago will impact you in ways you cannot fully imagine. This is a gift. It means your journey will be one of discovery, revelation, and wonder.

The path ahead will lead you through beautiful landscapes, past villages frozen in time, and into majestic cathedrals. If you allow it, it will also lead you into the truth of your heart. This journal is designed to be a companion on that journey. While your internal Camino may lead you through places of loss, confusion, doubt, and tears, if you are open to the journey, it will eventually bring you to a place of blessings, strength and joy. Let Psalm 84:5-7 be a blessing over you:

> Blessed are those whose strength is in you,
>   whose hearts are set on pilgrimage.
> As they pass through the Valley of Tears,
>   they make it a place of springs;
>   the autumn rains also cover it with pools.
> They go from strength to strength,
>   till each appears before God in Zion.

As you make your way to Santiago, may the Lord bless you and keep you. May the Lord make his face shine on you and be gracious to you. May the Lord turn his face toward you and give you peace. Buen Camino!

ANTICIPATION
The Eve of Your Pilgrimage

Tomorrow you set out towards Santiago. The truth is you already have been walking this path as you envisioned and prepared for this journey. In the morning, what up till now has only been a future hope will become reality. It would not be uncommon for you to feel both excitement and insecurity. You cannot wait to take your first steps, but you wonder if you will be able to make it. While these thoughts are to be expected, do not give them much attention. Instead, spend this time reflecting on what has brought you to this moment.

In the morning you start walking, but where did this journey really begin? When was the first time you remember the seed of the Camino being planted in you? What about that moment called to your heart? What hopes did it give birth to? What do you long to find as you make your way towards Santiago?

This journey has not only taken place in your heart. You have invested energy, time, and resources to make this pilgrimage possible. Reflect on what it has taken for you to come to this place. Celebrate the milestones you have already passed by as you planned and prepared to be here. Take time to acknowledge, and express gratitude for all the gifts that went into your being able to take this pilgrimage.

Finally, recognize you are in a liminal space between all that it took to arrive here, and what tomorrow will require. Wait, trust, listen, rest, and be thankful, for tomorrow you begin.

Reflections on the Day

Where did I begin today?

Where will I stay this evening?

How far have I come?

Where did beauty, kindness or generosity surprise me?

What was I thinking about or feeling?

Where did I encounter God?

Where did I most clearly see the truth of my own heart?

What is the state of my heart right now?

Other insights:

Take a few moments of prayerful silence. Use this time as an opportunity to express gratitude for the day, and ask for what you need. Trust God cares about what is on your heart and desires to meet you here.

RHYTHM

Day One

As you set out today, you will be tempted to measure yourself against others and your own expectations. Remind yourself this is not a competition. You may have to tell yourself this multiple times in the first few days on the Camino. As others pass you on the trail, you may feel the pressure to pick up the pace. When you pass your fellow pilgrims it may give you a feeling of being superior. Do not allow yourself to *entertain* either of these thoughts. They are traps and keep you from the real work at the beginning of this journey, discovering your own rhythm and pace.

Listen to your body. It will inform you of the speed at which you are to travel. Many pilgrims struggle in these first few days because they do not listen well to their bodies. Do not be afraid to take the time to stop to readjust your backpack or to retie your shoes. If your feet feel as if you are pounding them into the ground, walk slower. If your knees are aching from the downhill sections of the trail, reduce your speed. Your body will thank you tomorrow.

When conflict arises between your aspirations and your body, use it as an opportunity to explore what is pushing your desire to override what your body is telling you is best. What is going on in your heart when this happens? What are you being invited to release? What are you being challenged to embrace? What would it be to allow yourself to find your own cadence, and not compare your pace to others?

Reflections on the Day

Where did I begin today?

Where will I stay this evening?

How far have I come?

Where did beauty, kindness or generosity surprise me?

What was I thinking about or feeling?

Where did I encounter God?

Where did I most clearly see the truth of my own heart?

What is the state of my heart right now?

Other insights:

Take a few moments of prayerful silence. Use this time as an opportunity to express gratitude for the day, and ask for what you need. Trust God cares about what is on your heart and desires to meet you here.

ATTENTIVENESS
Day Two

While gaining altitude can cause your lungs to burn and your muscles to ache, the descents require you to be attentive. With every stride comes the potential of a fall and injury. This is made even more difficult when the path is covered in mud or loose stones. A serious slip or a twisted ankle is a real possibility. To avoid such hazards you will need to watch where you place each step. Your mind will naturally block out distraction to focus on where you are setting your feet. Allow this physical and mental exercise to become a training in attentiveness.

You will have an opportunity as the days pass to take this ability to focus your attention and move it from the physical to the relational. Just as you are aware of each step on the descents, begin being aware of the people who surround you as you make your way along the Camino. What is your posture towards them? What is the state of their hearts? Why do you think they have been brought across your path? What can they teach you? What are you able to give to them? These are all important questions.

As you encounter the physical and the relational aspects of this journey, be attentive to what is going on in your own heart. How is your heart adjusting to this new experience and the flexibility it requires? What is it that you need to embrace? What brings you joy? What bugs you? What are the fears, burdens, losses, longings, and hopes that you are carrying with you? Be attentive to what God and the experience of your journey may be speaking to you about these things.

Reflections on the Day

Where did I begin today?

Where will I stay this evening?

How far have I come?

Where did beauty, kindness or generosity surprise me?

What was I thinking about or feeling?

Where did I encounter God?

Where did I most clearly see the truth of my own heart?

What is the state of my heart right now?

Other insights:

Take a few moments of prayerful silence. Use this time as an opportunity to express gratitude for the day, and ask for what you need. Trust God cares about what is on your heart and desires to meet you here.

BURDENS
Day Three

By now you may have noticed tables in the Albergues displaying discarded items other pilgrims have chosen to leave behind. Though these things seemed important to bring at one time, now they have been deemed as unnecessary, because of the burden of their weight and the pain it causes. Resist the temptation to pick anything up. Instead, ask yourself, is there something you should remove from your pack and leave at one of these tables?

More importantly, what emotional or relational burdens have you brought with you to the Camino that may need to be dumped? What questions, worries or anxieties have you been carrying which have been weighing you down? Use today as an opportunity to rummage through the backpack of your heart and mind. Identify and acknowledge any burdens which have seemed to be important to hold on to, but now you recognize as keeping you from walking in lightness and freedom. Be willing to leave them behind.

Discarding these weights may feel like it is going to cost you something significant. Ask yourself, what price are you paying by carrying them? Imagine what it would feel like to walk without this weight. As a physical representation, carry a good sized stone for a kilometer today, feel its weight and the discomfort of holding on to it, and then choose to leave it alongside the path. When you do, also cast off the burdens you no longer wish to carry. You may want to turn to God and ask for His help in leaving them behind.

Reflections on the Day

Where did I begin today?

Where will I stay this evening?

How far have I come?

Where did beauty, kindness or generosity surprise me?

What was I thinking about or feeling?

Where did I encounter God?

Where did I most clearly see the truth of my own heart?

What is the state of my heart right now?

Other insights:

Take a few moments of prayerful silence. Use this time as an opportunity to express gratitude for the day, and ask for what you need. Trust God cares about what is on your heart and desires to meet you here.

STORY
Day Four

Your first days on the Camino have given you the opportunity to get to know a few of your fellow pilgrims. Some have immediately endeared themselves to you. Others may have been a bit of an irritation. What you are responding to is not just who you are experiencing, but the sum total of their story and how it has molded and shaped them. But it is not only their story you are learning about in the interaction. How the narrative of their life bumps into yours reveals something about your own heart and story.

As you walk today, hold your fellow sojourners, who you easily embrace, in your thoughts. From your experience of them, what do you know about their story? What draws you to them? What about their character, personality or perspective do you find attractive? What does this reveal and affirm about your own story?

Also, think about those who are more difficult to love. What is it about them that pushes your buttons? What story might lie behind the characteristics which bother you? What difference would it make in how you react if you knew this personality trait or behavior came from a place of brokenness rather than selfishness or arrogance? How could you more fully embrace their story? What change would this make in how you see them?

Finally, think about how these people can help you understand your own story. What does your openness, or lack thereof, to others reveal about how your life experience has molded and shaped you?

Reflections on the Day

Where did I begin today?

Where will I stay this evening?

How far have I come?

Where did beauty, kindness or generosity surprise me?

What was I thinking about or feeling?

Where did I encounter God?

Where did I most clearly see the truth of my own heart?

What is the state of my heart right now?

Other insights:

Take a few moments of prayerful silence. Use this time as an opportunity to express gratitude for the day, and ask for what you need. Trust God cares about what is on your heart and desires to meet you here.

EXPECTATIONS
Day Five

From the time the desire to walk the Camino was birthed in you, expectations began to form. You imagined what it would be like to walk along the path, converse with other pilgrims, and establish a daily routine. You anticipated what it would look and feel like. You had ideas about the way people would treat one another and the experiences you would share. You probably even had some vision of how you would respond to the experience of walking the Camino.

Some of what you envisioned has come to pass. This is a gift. Other expectations have not been met. This too is a gift. For in our disappointment, we are given the opportunity to learn to hold all things loosely. It is not wrong to have expectations, but unmet expectation can lead to frustration, anger and bitterness, if they are not held with open hands. This can cloud our vision, preventing us from seeing the good that is present and which often shows up in surprising ways.

As you walk today, meditate on the expectations you brought with you to the Camino. Which ones have been fulfilled? Take time to express gratitude for these. Where have you experienced disappointment? How has this affected your ability to be present to yourself and others? How is it affecting your experience?

Acknowledge these unmet expectations and choose to let them go. Allow the space which is created to enable you to be open to the unexpected gifts you may encounter as you make your way along the path.

Reflections on the Day

Where did I begin today?

Where will I stay this evening?

How far have I come?

Where did beauty, kindness or generosity surprise me?

What was I thinking about or feeling?

Where did I encounter God?

Where did I most clearly see the truth of my own heart?

What is the state of my heart right now?

Other insights:

Take a few moments of prayerful silence. Use this time as an opportunity to express gratitude for the day, and ask for what you need. Trust God cares about what is on your heart and desires to meet you here.

HUMILITY
Day Six

The Camino invites us to take a posture of humility. Humility may be best defined as seeing ourselves accurately. If you allow it, the journey to Santiago will help you to discover the truth of who you are mentally, emotionally, physically and spiritually. It will also, if you are willing, open you up to the presence of a loving God who has bestowed great value and worth upon you. Embracing this truth is a humbling experience. Knowing who you are and having the humility to embrace yourself as you are, gives you the capacity to interact with others without having to prove or protect anything.

While culture seems to extol pride and arrogance as the pathway to autonomy, it is the humble that are truly free. They are free to love regardless of how others respond. They are free to be who they are without having to hide or pretend, and they are free to fulfill their purpose because they know what they have been gifted to do.

As you walk today, seek to see yourself rightly. What gifts, capacities, and personality traits have you been given with which you are to bless the world? What weakness, needs, and limitations do you have which open the door for others to bless you? In what ways do you attempt to deny or hide these things? How willing are you to accept the truth of who you are? What part of who you are would you desire to embrace more fully? Thank God for who He has uniquely made you to be, and what he has created you to do. Own these things as good gifts. Choose to walk in humility today.

Reflections on the Day

Where did I begin today?

Where will I stay this evening?

How far have I come?

Where did beauty, kindness or generosity surprise me?

What was I thinking about or feeling?

Where did I encounter God?

Where did I most clearly see the truth of my own heart?

What is the state of my heart right now?

Other insights:

Take a few moments of prayerful silence. Use this time as an opportunity to express gratitude for the day, and ask for what you need. Trust God cares about what is on your heart and desires to meet you here.

REST
Day Seven

At the end of the day your body is begging to rest. This is especially true if you have pushed yourself and not stopped along the way. This kind of unyielding pace promotes blisters and overuse injuries. The wise pilgrim accepts their body's need for rest and builds in breaks throughout the day. These moments not only allow your body to rejuvenate, they help you to accept the fact that you are a finite being, who has limitations and who has needs. Culture sees acknowledging this truth as weakness, but in reality it is the pathway to tapping into the strength which is necessary for this journey. Rest is where strength is built. You tear a muscle down by lifting weights, but it is rest which rebuilds and strengthens.

Resting may be a struggle for you. You are not alone. We resist rest, because we do not trust. We do not trust that our identity is secure and it does not matter how quickly we move or how much distance we travel. We do not trust what we need will be waiting for us, even if we arrive later than expected. We do not trust that in resting we actually receive what is necessary to continue on the journey. Because we do not trust we strive. Cease striving.

Refusing to rest fatigues our bodies, stresses our minds, and causes our souls to be anxious. Is rest a rhythm you embrace? If not, what effect does this have on you? Where do you have difficulty trusting? Look for invitations to rest. Accepting these is as important as making it to your destination. Allow opportunities to rest to heighten your awareness of what is going on internally and around you.

Reflections on the Day

Where did I begin today?

Where will I stay this evening?

How far have I come?

Where did beauty, kindness or generosity surprise me?

What was I thinking about or feeling?

Where did I encounter God?

Where did I most clearly see the truth of my own heart?

What is the state of my heart right now?

Other insights:

Take a few moments of prayerful silence. Use this time as an opportunity to express gratitude for the day, and ask for what you need. Trust God cares about what is on your heart and desires to meet you here.

KNOWN
Day Eight

One of the deepest desires of the human heart is to be known and accepted. One of our greatest fears is to be exposed and rejected. This fear causes us to present a false self to others which we believe will be more acceptable, rather than the truth of who we really are. Making this move prevents us from having one of our deepest desires met. If we want to have our desire to be known and accepted fulfilled, we must be willing to take the risk of sharing the truth of who we are. We must share our history, successes and hopes, as well as our weaknesses, insecurities, fears and failures. Would you be willing to do this if you knew it would lead to being known?

To be known by others, we must first know ourselves. As you travel along the way today, meditate on who you really are. Hold both the things which you would have no problems sharing with others, as well as those things you keep hidden.

Often hidden things have power because we keep them in the dark. There is a risk in sharing them for sure, but what freedom might be found if you took the risk of bringing them into the light by sharing them with someone else? What bondage might be broken? What might it feel like to be fully known and accepted?

One of the gifts of the Camino is the opportunity to practice being known. Look for an opportunity today to risk being open. Not the whole, but at least a part of your story. The experience of it may be a turning point in your journey.

Reflections on the Day

Where did I begin today?

Where will I stay this evening?

How far have I come?

Where did beauty, kindness or generosity surprise me?

What was I thinking about or feeling?

Where did I encounter God?

Where did I most clearly see the truth of my own heart?

What is the state of my heart right now?

Other insights:

Take a few moments of prayerful silence. Use this time as an opportunity to express gratitude for the day, and ask for what you need. Trust God cares about what is on your heart and desires to meet you here.

MIRACLES
Day Nine

You will hear many stories of miracles on the way to Santiago. Some people have come searching for one. Maybe you have too. The miracles we seek often involve healing - mentally, emotionally, physically. What, if any, miracle do you seek? As you make your way today, take time to pray about what is on your heart. Cry out if necessary. Do not be afraid to ask for what you seek.

Miracles often do not appear exactly as we imagine they will. We may even fail to see them because they do not meet our expectations. Because we cannot see, does not mean they are not real or that we are not in the process of receiving one. The best ways to learn to see a miracle in the present is to look back and recognize how they have taken place in the past. Where have you experienced healing? How has your wounded heart been mended? How has clarity been brought to your distorted thinking? Where has a broken relationship been restored? Where are you now pain free, where you once had severe injury? Meditate on what brought healing to these places.

Now that you are holding these things, bring back into view the circumstances where you desire to receive healing. From your experience, by what process do you think healing will come? Often healing requires a willingness to wait and to trust. Trust allows us to be grateful even before the miracle appears. Spend time expressing gratitude for both what you are learning in the midst of this suffering and for the healing which will take place. How does it feel to bring your heart to this place?

Reflections on the Day

Where did I begin today?

Where will I stay this evening?

How far have I come?

Where did beauty, kindness or generosity surprise me?

What was I thinking about or feeling?

Where did I encounter God?

Where did I most clearly see the truth of my own heart?

What is the state of my heart right now?

Other insights:

Take a few moments of prayerful silence. Use this time as an opportunity to express gratitude for the day, and ask for what you need. Trust God cares about what is on your heart and desires to meet you here.

44

GRATITUDE
Day Ten

Gratitude is one of the most powerful expressions of the heart. When life is going well, it acknowledges what we have received is a gift. But it does more than make note of the ways we have been blessed. Practicing gratitude strengthens us physically, emotionally and spiritually. It makes us healthier and happier, and it trains us to be able to recognize gifts, even in the difficult circumstances in life. What benefits do you recognize in your life from cultivating a thankful heart?

Chances are, as you have been walking you have come across people who have a well-developed capacity for gratitude. How did it feel to be with these folks? It is equally as likely you have met those who seemed to struggle to be thankful, even in the best situations. What was it like to keep their company? More importantly, which kind of person are you?

The Camino is rich with opportunity to develop your capacity for gratefulness. Meditate on what you have experienced on your journey and spend time prayerfully expressing gratitude for the gifts you have received. Pay particular attention to the difficult situations which come to mind. Seek to identify how you might be able to see these as gifts. This is a powerful way to redeem what might otherwise be viewed as bad.

Be open to opportunities which present themselves to share the things you are thankful for. Say thank you often, and store up reminders by keeping a list in your journal of the gifts you have received.

Reflections on the Day

Where did I begin today?

Where will I stay this evening?

How far have I come?

Where did beauty, kindness or generosity surprise me?

What was I thinking about or feeling?

Where did I encounter God?

Where did I most clearly see the truth of my own heart?

What is the state of my heart right now?

Other insights:

Take a few moments of prayerful silence. Use this time as an opportunity to express gratitude for the day, and ask for what you need. Trust God cares about what is on your heart and desires to meet you here.

LOSS
Day Eleven

The Camino intensifies the experience of relational loss. At home, people move out of your life in seasons, years, or even decades. Here, they can enter and move in and out in a matter of hours, days and if you are lucky, weeks. If you have thoroughly enjoyed their company, broke bread together, and shared the deep things of your heart it is hard to watch them walk ahead, or leave them behind. These experiences can come in quick succession and it can be hard on the heart. It is also a gift, and can teach us a life-giving posture to help us navigate loss in any aspect of our lives.

The first move is to acknowledge it for what it is. It is a loss. This will not be true of everyone you meet, but with some you may feel this very deeply. It is good to grieve what has been lost. It acknowledges the value the relationship has had and the imprint it has made on your life. Grief is a form of celebration. We should not let the sadness keep us from it. What losses do you already need to grieve as you have walked?

Loss also brings with it relational space which can now be filled with someone new. Will you dare imagine the person who is about to walk into your story might bring with them something important and necessary? Learn to grieve, but also learn to hold the future with anticipation, trusting the people you are about to meet will bring new life, in surprising ways, at just the right moment. How can you walk with a posture of anticipation, even as you grieve the loss of those you must leave?

Reflections on the Day

Where did I begin today?

Where will I stay this evening?

How far have I come?

Where did beauty, kindness or generosity surprise me?

What was I thinking about or feeling?

Where did I encounter God?

Where did I most clearly see the truth of my own heart?

What is the state of my heart right now?

Other insights:

Take a few moments of prayerful silence. Use this time as an opportunity to express gratitude for the day, and ask for what you need. Trust God cares about what is on your heart and desires to meet you here.

LOVED
Day Twelve

The best type of love, maybe the only genuine kind of love, is the love we do not have to earn, but which is freely lavished upon us. Many struggle believing they can be loved like this. The world, the enemy of our soul, and sometimes our own internal voice point to our failures, character defects, and insecurities and whisper to our hearts, *because of these things you are not loved*. This is a lie and we need to treat it as such.

You have great value and worth. This does not come from what you do. It cannot be stripped from you because of what you have done. The Creator has bestowed upon you his divine imprint and paid an infinite price to make you aware of how dearly loved you are. How easy is it for you to accept this truth? What lies would have to be discarded to walk in this reality?

Embracing this truth will give you the freedom to see yourself as you really are. There is no fear, because even your darkest secret does not change the fact that you are loved. Knowing and walking in this reality enables us to live authentic, loving, powerful lives.

Today, remind yourself that you are fully loved. Allow this truth to form how you see yourself and interact with others. Knowing you are loved, centering yourself on this truth, gives you the capacity to love others regardless of what they do or what they have done. This is complete freedom. Look for opportunities to love like this today. Notice how doing so impacts others and leads your own heart to embrace being loved.

Reflections on the Day

Where did I begin today?

Where will I stay this evening?

How far have I come?

Where did beauty, kindness or generosity surprise me?

What was I thinking about or feeling?

Where did I encounter God?

Where did I most clearly see the truth of my own heart?

What is the state of my heart right now?

Other insights:

Take a few moments of prayerful silence. Use this time as an opportunity to express gratitude for the day, and ask for what you need. Trust God cares about what is on your heart and desires to meet you here.

WILDERNESS
Day Thirteen

In spiritual writings, the wilderness often represents a place of purgation, consecration and commissioning. It is also a place of contemplation, awareness and vision. Do not be afraid to enter the wilderness as you walk. Open yourself to what this space can reveal about what needs to be purged, set apart and given purpose before you can step into your life's calling.

In some ways, the Camino will act as a boundary marker between where you have come from and where you are going. As you walk, become aware of what you may want to purge from your life in preparation to move forward. As you walk, meditate on those things which may have been useful at one time, but now seem obsolete. Acknowledge them for the help they provided in the previous season, celebrate them, and then let them go.

Where we have been has a great influence on where we are called to go in the future. Take time to also reflect on what the past has to speak to you regarding your purpose moving forward. What passions have been cultivated? What have you been uniquely shaped and gifted to do?

How could you honor these things by setting yourself apart for the purpose they reveal?

The picture of your future, which the answers to these questions will help to paint, may take time to appear. Do not be concerned if it does not materialize quickly. Instead, allow the wilderness to be a time where you hold these things, trusting as you do awareness and clarity will come.

Reflections on the Day

Where did I begin today?

Where will I stay this evening?

How far have I come?

Where did beauty, kindness or generosity surprise me?

What was I thinking about or feeling?

Where did I encounter God?

Where did I most clearly see the truth of my own heart?

What is the state of my heart right now?

Other insights:

Take a few moments of prayerful silence. Use this time as an opportunity to express gratitude for the day, and ask for what you need. Trust God cares about what is on your heart and desires to meet you here.

EMOTIONS
Day Fourteen

Some people want to deny their emotions, so they ignore or stuff down what they feel. This energy goes somewhere. Either it squirts out sideways, or it erupts when the pressure gets to be too much. Others allow their emotions to control them. They are blown back and forth depending on how they feel. This can be unsettling and make them feel out of control, which just pours fuel on the fire. How do you relate to your emotions?

Emotions are a gift. They should not be ignored, nor should they control our lives. Instead, emotions should be seen as a barometer which reveals the condition of our heart and soul. They give us a good sense of what is going on inside, and invite us to explore what might be behind what we are feeling.

While it may not seem necessary to analyze our positive emotions, taking the time to understand why we are feeling good helps us to understand the needs, expectations, and desires of our heart. Noticing when these are being met helps us to discern what might be at the root of negative emotions we feel when they go unfulfilled. Allowing our emotions to lead us to our unmet expectations and desires enables us to identify and then attend to them in helpful, life-giving ways.

As you walk today, notice what you are feeling. Name the emotion. What is this feeling revealing about the state of your heart? What expectation, need or desire might be behind what you feel? How could you respond to this in a way that is helpful to your soul?

Reflections on the Day

Where did I begin today?

Where will I stay this evening?

How far have I come?

Where did beauty, kindness or generosity surprise me?

What was I thinking about or feeling?

Where did I encounter God?

Where did I most clearly see the truth of my own heart?

What is the state of my heart right now?

Other insights:

Take a few moments of prayerful silence. Use this time as an opportunity to express gratitude for the day, and ask for what you need. Trust God cares about what is on your heart and desires to meet you here.

HEAT
Day Fifteen

When we experience painful wounds or difficult circumstances, it can feel like the sun beating down upon us in a land where we have no hope of finding shade. It can sap our energy, slow our pace, and cause us to long for relief. These hard places can also be a gift, revealing the true substance of our own hearts. A famous preacher, Charles Spurgeon, once said, "The same sun which melts wax hardens clay." What has been the effect of the wounds and difficulties of your life? Have they hardened your heart, or have they melted away its resistance to discovering the truth contained in these hard places?

Be open, today, to the reality of your heart and the posture it has taken towards the hurtful experiences of your life. How do you feel about what you see? What is the impact has this posture on your life and relationships?

Recall one circumstance or event which seems to have caused you to harden your heart. Spend time reviewing this in your mind. Allow yourself to feel whatever comes up. Notice what effect this has had on how you relate to others and God. Walk in the truth of these things.

When ready, explore what it would be like to allow your heart to soften in relationship to this circumstance. Are there any fears associated with this thought? If you pushed past these fears, what would it open you to, which you are now closed off from? Dare to imagine the sun's heat melting away the negative impact of any hardness of heart you have developed. Soften your heart to the truth you may learn and the freedom you may discover.

Reflections on the Day

Where did I begin today?

Where will I stay this evening?

How far have I come?

Where did beauty, kindness or generosity surprise me?

What was I thinking about or feeling?

Where did I encounter God?

Where did I most clearly see the truth of my own heart?

What is the state of my heart right now?

Other insights:

Take a few moments of prayerful silence. Use this time as an opportunity to express gratitude for the day, and ask for what you need. Trust God cares about what is on your heart and desires to meet you here.

SURRENDER
Day Sixteen

Most of us do not like the thought of surrender. It carries with it the idea of weakness and defeat. It means being stripped of our freedom and defenses. It is the capitulation of our will, to the will of another. Why would anyone want to surrender?

But what if surrendering is actually the most freeing act our will can exercise? What if in giving up control, we discover the ability to not be ruled by what happens to us? We would not be yielding to the will of another, but liberating ourselves from it. Maybe we would discover, for the very first time, what it is to be truly free.

What have you been invited to surrender as you have been walking? Is it the need to have what you do define who you are? Is it the propensity to have how others react and respond to you affect your state of being? Is it the habit of having what you own determine your value? Is it the tendency to measure yourself against others, in order to feel better about who you are? Is it is the inability to look past your faults and failures and embrace the fact you are loved?

All these ways of thinking keep you in bondage. What consequences do you experience from carrying these chains? What would it be to lay them off? The key is surrendering the ways you have filtered the world and your worth. Open yourself to the reality you are loved regardless of what you do or own, how others react or respond, or how you are seen or see yourself. Embracing this love allows you to walk in freedom and strength.

Reflections on the Day

Where did I begin today?

Where will I stay this evening?

How far have I come?

Where did beauty, kindness or generosity surprise me?

What was I thinking about or feeling?

Where did I encounter God?

Where did I most clearly see the truth of my own heart?

What is the state of my heart right now?

Other insights:

Take a few moments of prayerful silence. Use this time as an opportunity to express gratitude for the day, and ask for what you need. Trust God cares about what is on your heart and desires to meet you here.

CELEBRATION
Day Seventeen

You have either just crossed the halfway point of your journey or you will come to it in the next few days. This is reason to celebrate. You have been able to push past the uncertainty and pain of the first few days. You have endured blisters, backaches and a cacophony of snoring pilgrims. You have found your rhythm and made your way nearly 400 kilometers along the Camino de Santiago. This is quite an accomplishment, and no matter what happens from here, it is worth celebrating.

Celebration is as important of a discipline as looking inward at our own heart and motive, or looking outward to love and serve. It is an opportunity to recognize the good which you have received, to acknowledge the giver of good gifts and to invite others to share in your joy. Who would not want to be part of that party?

Celebration protects us from becoming negative or cynical. It forces our hearts to remember the good we can so easily forget, especially when we still have 400 kilometers before us, or when life continues to present us with challenges. It is a rhythm which is good for our soul.

At this point in your journey, what do you have to celebrate? As you walk, make a mental list of the blessings you have experienced along the way and in life. How can you celebrate these things? How can you invite others to share in the festivities? It could be as simple as a toast as you gather around the dinner table tonight, or as creative as making a special meal to share. Whatever the case, today, exercise the discipline of celebration.

Reflections on the Day

Where did I begin today?

Where will I stay this evening?

How far have I come?

Where did beauty, kindness or generosity surprise me?

What was I thinking about or feeling?

Where did I encounter God?

74

Where did I most clearly see the truth of my own heart?

What is the state of my heart right now?

Other insights:

*Take a few moments of prayerful silence. Use this time as an
opportunity to express gratitude for the day, and ask for what
you need. Trust God cares about what is on your heart and
desires to meet you here.*

KINDNESS
Day Eighteen

There may be no other character quality which is more underrated and more needed than kindness. Kindness has the capacity to ease the pain of the injured, chase away loneliness, bestow a sense of worth and value, increase joy and build community. It enriches the lives of both the giver and the recipient. Kindness often costs nothing, but can mean everything.

You cannot have gotten this far into the Camino without having had some experience of kindness. Someone may have bestowed it upon you, you may have witnessed it being presented to someone else, or you may have been the one to confer it on another. Whatever the case, take some time today to think about how these acts of kindness impacted the people and changed the tone of the interaction. What feelings come up when you think about the effects of these acts of kindness?

Allow your meditation on kindness to open your eyes to seeing opportunities to express kindness to the people you will meet today. A warm smile can communicate kindness. An act of service, a thoughtful gesture, a well-placed word of encouragement or sharing of what you have can all be powerful expressions of kindness. Maybe, one of the kindest things you can do for someone today is to simply be with them and listen for a period of time.

When the opportunity to be kind presents itself, seize it. Take time to notice the effect it has on the recipient. Also, be aware of how it impacts your own heart. How does it make you feel to be a purveyor of kindness?

Reflections on the Day

Where did I begin today?

Where will I stay this evening?

How far have I come?

Where did beauty, kindness or generosity surprise me?

What was I thinking about or feeling?

Where did I encounter God?

Where did I most clearly see the truth of my own heart?

What is the state of my heart right now?

Other insights:

Take a few moments of prayerful silence. Use this time as an opportunity to express gratitude for the day, and ask for what you need. Trust God cares about what is on your heart and desires to meet you here.

80

DIVERSITY
Day Nineteen

As they move towards Santiago, the Camino unites people from all around the world in a common experience and purpose. This in no way negates the differences in culture, religion, and social backgrounds of the people who walk together. This diversity is a gift, and there is an opportunity on this route to experience the richness of our differences unlike anywhere else in the world. Make the most of it. Allow it to expand your world and open your heart to the beauty of the uniqueness of each person.

Today, be intentional about getting to know someone from another country. You may already be walking with a person who comes from a place other than your own. Get to know them at an even deeper level. Engage in conversations which allow you to explore the cultures which have formed you. How are they different? How are they the same? Talk about how where you are from has shaped the way you think. Share how you celebrate important events and milestones in life. What might you want to borrow from their culture to make your celebrations more enjoyable or significant? There is so much to explore. Allow curiosity to guide you.

When you find yourself walking alone, take time to be mindful of what you have discovered. Did the experience change your perception of the person, their country or the world? Did it reveal anything to you about the filter through which you see the world? What will you take away from this conversation? Simply enjoy the chance to get to know someone who is different from you.

Reflections on the Day

Where did I begin today?

Where will I stay this evening?

How far have I come?

Where did beauty, kindness or generosity surprise me?

What was I thinking about or feeling?

Where did I encounter God?

Where did I most clearly see the truth of my own heart?

_____

_____

_____

_____

What is the state of my heart right now?

_____

_____

_____

_____

Other insights:

_____

_____

_____

_____

_____

_____

_____

_____

_____

_____

Take a few moments of prayerful silence. Use this time as an opportunity to express gratitude for the day, and ask for what you need. Trust God cares about what is on your heart and desires to meet you here.

SERENDIPITY
Day Twenty

While you spent months of planning to walk the Camino and you begin each morning with a modicum of expectations for what the day will hold, it is the serendipity of the experience which will produce some of the most rich and meaningful moments and interactions. Do not allow the plans you have made or the goals you have set for the day to rob you of the joy of finding good things in unforeseen places and people.

You may have already had several experiences of serendipity, a chance meeting with a person who spoke what you needed to hear, finding something you were hoping for when you least expected it, or having a person you enjoyed, who walked away a few days earlier, show back up. These are gifts which can be missed if you hold too rigidly to your predetermined ambitions and plans.

How tightly do you hold to these things? Having an idea of where you desire to go and how you will go about getting there is important, even necessary if you want to move forward. But, it is equally essential to hold these things lightly, trusting when circumstances do not go according to plan, they may lead you to something you could not have foreseen or imagined which is even better. What would it take for you to be open to this, especially now that your daily rhythm is fairly well established?

When your routine is disrupted and your plans get pushed, allow these things to be a reminder to look expectantly for what good thing may serendipitously show up. Be mindful of your openness and flexibility.

Reflections on the Day

Where did I begin today?

Where will I stay this evening?

How far have I come?

Where did beauty, kindness or generosity surprise me?

What was I thinking about or feeling?

Where did I encounter God?

Where did I most clearly see the truth of my own heart?

What is the state of my heart right now?

Other insights:

Take a few moments of prayerful silence. Use this time as an opportunity to express gratitude for the day, and ask for what you need. Trust God cares about what is on your heart and desires to meet you here.

HURT

Day Twenty-One

We do not like to admit when we have been hurt. When we fall, we jump back up quickly and assure those who might be watching, "I am alright." When someone wounds us deeply, we deny their words or actions impacted us as significantly as they did because we do not want to appear weak. If the trauma happened in childhood, the adults around us may not have had the capacity to help us process it in ways which would have been helpful. We may have learned to bury the pain.

This would be fine, except hurt, especially hurt which has not been acknowledged or felt, continues to affect our lives long after the bruises have disappeared, or memory of the trauma has faded. It shapes the way we relate to others, and how open we are to the world. How has your hurt affected your relationships and openness?

Will you accept the invitation to think about just one significant hurt you have experienced? This is a brave move, which can lead to freedom. What happened to you? How would you define the hurt which you experienced? Name it and acknowledge it for what it is. Be open to the emotions which surround this injury. How did you feel then? How do you feel about it now? Can you give yourself permission to experience these feelings? Do so.

Sometimes, we can feel as if we are defined by the hurt which has been inflicted upon us. Remind yourself this is something that happened to you. It is not who you are. See your hurt in light of this truth and when you have seen it for what it is, put it in its right place.

Reflections on the Day

Where did I begin today?

Where will I stay this evening?

How far have I come?

Where did beauty, kindness or generosity surprise me?

What was I thinking about or feeling?

Where did I encounter God?

Where did I most clearly see the truth of my own heart?

What is the state of my heart right now?

Other insights:

Take a few moments of prayerful silence. Use this time as an opportunity to express gratitude for the day, and ask for what you need. Trust God cares about what is on your heart and desires to meet you here.

FORGIVENESS
Day Twenty-Two

Someone once said unforgiveness is like drinking poison and waiting for the other person to die. They are right. Unforgiveness is a caustic concoction which eats away at your physical, emotional and spiritual health, while often leaving the other person untouched and unaware of the hurt, anger and bitterness you are carrying. Why do this to yourself?

We struggle to extend forgiveness because we think it excuses what happened. It does not. We fear it will mean what happened did not matter. It matters greatly. We feel like it will mean denying how the offense affected us. It does not mean this at all. We think forgiving will let the other person off the hook. It will not.

Forgiveness requires acknowledging what took place and how it impacted you. You then have the power to choose to let go of the offense, to cancel the debt which is owed. Forgiveness is releasing the right to punish the person. This is not letting them off the hook. It is allowing love to cover their sin. The debt owed is now owed to love. The relationship may or may not be restored, but your heart will be freed from the burden of unforgiveness.

The first move in forgiving others is remembering the pardon you have received. Think of a time when you were forgiven. What did it feel like to have the person let go of the offense? Consider where you are being invited to forgive. Acknowledge what happened. See it for what it is, and then choose to cover this offense with love and forgive.

Reflections on the Day

Where did I begin today?

Where will I stay this evening?

How far have I come?

Where did beauty, kindness or generosity surprise me?

What was I thinking about or feeling?

Where did I encounter God?

Where did I most clearly see the truth of my own heart?

What is the state of my heart right now?

Other insights:

Take a few moments of prayerful silence. Use this time as an opportunity to express gratitude for the day, and ask for what you need. Trust God cares about what is on your heart and desires to meet you here.

INDIFFERENCE
Day Twenty-Three

When you hear the word indifference, you probably think it means having an uncaring attitude. While this may be the modern interpretation of the word, it is not what the Desert Fathers were espousing when they called us to live a life of indifference. For them, it meant ordering your life in such a way that your decisions and responses were detached from the actions of others, your own ego driven desires, and from circumstance. This detachment allows us to abandon what is not necessary, including our internal reactions to the attitudes and opinions of others.

It is a powerful way to live, and it opens us up to the possibility of loving others, regardless of how they treat or react to you. Indifference enables you to love more fully and care more deeply than is otherwise possible. It gives independence and freedom to your love that is not possible when it is attached to the response of others. It is what gives birth to a love which knows no bounds.

Have you ever loved like this? What did it feel like? Have you ever experienced this kind of love? To grow in the ability to love regardless, ask yourself, how attached is your love to the desires of your own heart, the responses and reactions of others, or the circumstances of your life? What might you need to willingly detach from in order to be indifferent towards these things? How would this free you to express boundless love? What resistance do you have to making this move? What do you fear? Remember, perfect love casts out fear.

Reflections on the Day

Where did I begin today?

Where will I stay this evening?

How far have I come?

Where did beauty, kindness or generosity surprise me?

What was I thinking about or feeling?

Where did I encounter God?

Where did I most clearly see the truth of my own heart?

What is the state of my heart right now?

Other insights:

Take a few moments of prayerful silence. Use this time as an opportunity to express gratitude for the day, and ask for what you need. Trust God cares about what is on your heart and desires to meet you here.

RELEASE
Day Twenty-Four

As you have walked you have become aware of the burdens and fears you have carried with you, on the Camino and in life. You have recognized the places of woundedness and unforgiveness. You have been open to see yourself for who you really are, holding both the good and the bad, knowing you are loved in both. Seeing these things has been hard, but good. In acknowledging what is so, you have opened yourself to exploring how you feel, and how you have learned to deal with these things. You have also looked at how they have impacted the way you see yourself, others and God. This has been a significant journey.

From this place you now get to choose. What do you want to acknowledge and leave behind, and what do you desire to take with you? Do not rush through this opportunity to sift through these things. Allow yourself the internal space to let what is true to surface in your heart. What do you see floating to the top? What needs to be skimmed off and discarded? When you are ready, let go of what you do not need or want, and affirm who you are and are not.

Do not be afraid. In releasing these things you will discover what remains is more than enough for the journey ahead. In fact, you will discover, not carrying this weight will set you free to be who you have been created to be. You may desire to turn in prayer to the Spirit who guides us into all truth and ask for the strength needed to leave these burdens behind.

Reflections on the Day

Where did I begin today?

Where will I stay this evening?

How far have I come?

Where did beauty, kindness or generosity surprise me?

What was I thinking about or feeling?

Where did I encounter God?

Where did I most clearly see the truth of my own heart?

What is the state of my heart right now?

Other insights:

Take a few moments of prayerful silence. Use this time as an opportunity to express gratitude for the day, and ask for what you need. Trust God cares about what is on your heart and desires to meet you here.

AUTHENTICITY
Day Twenty-Five

Even though you have laid off so much on this journey, there will still be a temptation to present yourself as other than you really are. This propensity to cover and hide your authentic self is a struggle mankind has had from the beginning. It stems from the fear if others knew who you really are and what you have done, you will not be loved and accepted. This belief traps you behind the wall of a false self, which is erected to protect you from being rejected and unloved. Even if others affirm this inauthentic self, you will never feel fully loved, because you know it is not the real you that they are loving.

If, however, you take the risk of allowing others to know your authentic self and they respond with love, you will have an experience of love which will fill one of the most basic human desires, to be loved for who we are.

As you walk away from the things you have laid down, walk out from behind the wall of your false self. Allow others to know you as you really are. If you have opened yourself to the invitations to be known and loved along the way, you have already experienced the power of an authentic life. Do not give in to the temptation to pick up what you have just put down. Notice when you feel as if you are being inauthentic. What effect is this having on you? Also, be aware of when you are living authentically. How does this make you feel? Above all, give yourself grace. This is a journey of growth, not a destination, and over time, you will expand your capacity to recognize and share your genuine self.

Reflections on the Day

Where did I begin today?

Where will I stay this evening?

How far have I come?

Where did beauty, kindness or generosity surprise me?

What was I thinking about or feeling?

Where did I encounter God?

Where did I most clearly see the truth of my own heart?

What is the state of my heart right now?

Other insights:

Take a few moments of prayerful silence. Use this time as an opportunity to express gratitude for the day, and ask for what you need. Trust God cares about what is on your heart and desires to meet you here.

WONDER
Day Twenty-Six

Where have you encountered wonder? Maybe, it was when the sun peaked over the horizon and painted the clouds in pink and then golden hues, or when high on a ridge, you first caught sight of the path descending into a valley, weaving its way through a patchwork of fields. Perhaps, it was when you paused at dusk to delight in the long shadows and illumination of the golden hour. Wonder may have appeared in the dancing flowers at the edge of a barley field, the light glistening off the surface of a river, or in the fuzz from the cottonwood trees riding the wind. It may have been contained in the vaulted ceiling of a cathedral, the perfect timing of an act of kindness, or in the warm smile of a fellow pilgrim. I do not know when wonder captured your imagination, but I know it did.

The experience of wonder not only fills your heart and soul, it expands your ability to witness it. It is as if one moment of splendor, which takes your breath away, creates in you the aptitude to discover it in new places. Your capacity for wonder has grown as you have walked the Camino. This is to be cherished.

Wonder grabs your attention and engages your senses. It opens you to the sacred and makes you feel small, in the best sort of way. Wonder inspires and calls out the noblest part of your spirit. Pause in moments of wonder today. What about them speaks most significantly to your heart? What do they arouse in you? Take time to capture at least one in prose, a poem, or a photo. Allow the experience to enlarge your soul.

Reflections on the Day

Where did I begin today?

Where will I stay this evening?

How far have I come?

Where did beauty, kindness or generosity surprise me?

What was I thinking about or feeling?

Where did I encounter God?

Where did I most clearly see the truth of my own heart?

What is the state of my heart right now?

Other insights:

Take a few moments of prayerful silence. Use this time as an opportunity to express gratitude for the day, and ask for what you need. Trust God cares about what is on your heart and desires to meet you here.

PEACE
Day Twenty-Seven

Peace is not the absence of relational discord or difficulty in life. It is stillness or quietness of the heart regardless of what is taking place around you. This lack of inner turmoil is born in trust. You can exercise this kind of confidence when you know the foundation of your life has the capacity to hold secure, even when you are buffeted by strong winds and rain. It is a hope which acts as an anchor for our soul, keeping us from being tossed about by the circumstances of life.

You willingly enter into peace when you choose to trust at increasingly deeper levels. The ability to do this is born in the belief that God is good, desires good for you, and works for good in all things, even the hard places. No doubt, you have encountered this truth as you walk the Camino. A situation occurred which seemed anything but good in the moment, and as it worked itself out you discovered the outcome was a gift you had not foreseen or expected. In it you recognized God's goodness to you.

The Hebrew word for peace, shalom, carries with it the ideas of completeness, wholeness and unity. When used as a greeting, it is a blessing of restoration, fulfillment, well-being and security. How has your journey blessed you with peace? What has it enabled to be restored within you and in your relationship with God and others? What has it done to bring a greater sense of wholeness to your life? Where are you being invited to trust at a deeper level? Let this growing trust produce peace. Allow it to wash over your soul, and make your way secure.

Reflections on the Day

Where did I begin today?

Where will I stay this evening?

How far have I come?

Where did beauty, kindness or generosity surprise me?

What was I thinking about or feeling?

Where did I encounter God?

Where did I most clearly see the truth of my own heart?

What is the state of my heart right now?

Other insights:

Take a few moments of prayerful silence. Use this time as an opportunity to express gratitude for the day, and ask for what you need. Trust God cares about what is on your heart and desires to meet you here.

COMMUNION
Day Twenty-Eight

The sharing of a meal can be far more significant than merely eating with others. The breaking of bread and the pouring of wine can be an expression of unity and kinship. It has the potential to draw the people who occupy the space around the table into a community, which is built on shared experience, common hope, and the mutual affirmation of what is true. We join in this communion with one another when we engage in remembrance, celebration and anticipation. Hopefully, you have shared in a meal on the Camino that allowed you to engage in this kind of fellowship. If you have, how did it feel to experience this connection with others? What were the elements which made it possible? What were the things you shared with one another? How did this experience shape your interactions in the days which followed?

Today, you will have the opportunity to sit and eat with people. You can use this time to take in calories, or you can breathe significance into the occasion by being intentional about what takes place. Ask questions which open your experiences to one another. Celebrate the victories of the past few weeks. Remember the challenges. Notice the desires which unify your hearts. Raise your glasses and toast the truths you have been discovering along the way. Acknowledge the grace you have received and the fellowship you share. Laugh together. Be present with one another. Encourage each other. Recognize the presence of God.

Reflections on the Day

Where did I begin today?

Where will I stay this evening?

How far have I come?

Where did beauty, kindness or generosity surprise me?

What was I thinking about or feeling?

Where did I encounter God?

Where did I most clearly see the truth of my own heart?

What is the state of my heart right now?

Other insights:

Take a few moments of prayerful silence. Use this time as an opportunity to express gratitude for the day, and ask for what you need. Trust God cares about what is on your heart and desires to meet you here.

CAPACITY
Day Twenty-Nine

When something is hard and rigid, it has a limited capacity for what it can hold. Fill it too full and it will burst. On the other hand, if something is pliable and elastic, it has the capacity to expand. This flexibility enables it to grow and embrace what once seemed impossible for it to accommodate.

As you have walked the Camino you have been invited to acknowledge your story with all of its burdens, fears, pain, expectations, emotions, and unmet desires. This may have been uncomfortable, even painful at times. You may have felt as if you were going to burst, but you didn't.

You have also had the opportunity to affirm your story's joys, hopes, blessings, gratefulness, and experiences of being loved. This expanded your soul and created the space necessary to hold both parts of your story. This capacity is emotional maturity and it is good to recognize how much it has developed. Can you recognize how your soul has grown as you have made this journey?

As you walk today, be mindful of the growth that has taken place in your ability to be present to both sides of your story. Recognize the capacity which has been created. Ponder how this has changed you. Where do you feel it most? What are you now able to hold that you once thought could have caused you to burst? How will this growth in capacity affect you as you move forward? What good things might now fill this space? Rest in the knowledge, whatever may come, you now have increased capacity to hold it.

Reflections on the Day

Where did I begin today?

Where will I stay this evening?

How far have I come?

Where did beauty, kindness or generosity surprise me?

What was I thinking about or feeling?

Where did I encounter God?

Where did I most clearly see the truth of my own heart?

What is the state of my heart right now?

Other insights:

Take a few moments of prayerful silence. Use this time as an opportunity to express gratitude for the day, and ask for what you need. Trust God cares about what is on your heart and desires to meet you here.

BLESSING

Day Thirty

One of the deepest longings God has placed in the human heart is the desire to be blessed. To bless someone is to speak good into their life, wish for their well-being, and articulate your desire for their happiness. A blessing also declares favor upon a person, not for what they have done, but for who they are. It is a powerful act, which engenders feelings of acceptance, honor and respect to the one who is blessed.

When have you been blessed? Words of blessing may have been spoken over you by the influential people in your life like a parent, family member, teacher, coach or friend. They could also have come from someone you least expected to bless you. Try to think of a specific time you received a blessing. What did it feel like to hear those words? How did it affect the way you saw yourself, and the person who spoke them? What impact did it have on how you engaged the world?

Often, blessings take place at the big events of our lives like weddings, anniversaries, graduations and significant birthdays. As powerful as the act of blessing is, there is no reason why we should limit it to these occasions. Ask God to open your eyes to see a person who might need your blessing. Find a moment when it would be appropriate to speak good into their life, and declare favor over them. Your blessing, freely given, will honor and empower the one who receives it. Blessing has great power for good. Wield it with abandon. Watch its transformative power.

Reflections on the Day

Where did I begin today?

Where will I stay this evening?

How far have I come?

Where did beauty, kindness or generosity surprise me?

What was I thinking about or feeling?

Where did I encounter God?

Where did I most clearly see the truth of my own heart?

What is the state of my heart right now?

Other insights:

Take a few moments of prayerful silence. Use this time as an opportunity to express gratitude for the day, and ask for what you need. Trust God cares about what is on your heart and desires to meet you here.

PURPOSE
Day Thirty-One

Purpose gives direction and meaning to our lives. It helps us filter decisions and make choices. Maybe, part of the reason you chose to walk the Camino was to give yourself the space to be able to clarify your purpose. This may be especially true if you are standing at a crossroads in a period of transition.

Over the past thirty days your purpose has included reaching Santiago. Very shortly you will fulfill that part of your calling for this season of your life. Hopefully, this journey has helped you to explore, understand, and clarify who you have been made to be. This is far more significant than figuring out what kind of job you should have. It answers the deeper question of, what was I created to do?

As you have had time to be present to yourself, and open to the deepest longings of your heart, what has surfaced in regards to your purpose? What have your life experiences shaped and prepared you to do? Pay attention to your deepest passions and make note of those things which dissatisfy you. What do these reveal? Allow all of these things to help you discern your purpose. If you are having trouble defining your calling, ask yourself the question, "If I knew I would not fail what would I do?" Does your answer line up with who you are, where you have come from, and the gifts and capacities with which you have been blessed? Though it will continue to develop, how would you articulate your purpose? Be bold enough to share this with someone.

Reflections on the Day

Where did I begin today?

Where will I stay this evening?

How far have I come?

Where did beauty, kindness or generosity surprise me?

What was I thinking about or feeling?

Where did I encounter God?

Where did I most clearly see the truth of my own heart?

What is the state of my heart right now?

Other insights:

Take a few moments of prayerful silence. Use this time as an opportunity to express gratitude for the day, and ask for what you need. Trust God cares about what is on your heart and desires to meet you here.

LOVE
Day Thirty-Two

The people you have met along the way have given you the opportunity to exercise patience, kindness and humility. You have been able to choose to refrain from boasting, lay aside self-interest, be slow to anger, and honor others. There have been chances to demonstrate trust, hope and perseverance. Generosity has been offered as an alternative to envy, and you have had the option to rejoice in the truth you have discovered. Whether you recognize it or not, this is love. If you have availed yourself to the opportunities to practice these character qualities, you have grown in your capacity to express it.

As you reflect on your journey, where were you invited to love more completely? What resistance did you have to this invitation? Did you choose to love anyway? What was the result of pressing past this reluctance and demonstrating love? How did the love you expressed build up the one who received it? How did it impact you?

There are many good things with which to fill life. You can fill it with accomplishments, knowledge, wisdom, artistry, and even good deeds, but without love these things are nothing. You gain nothing. But, add love and they suddenly possess a power to impart life. Where have you witnessed the life made possible through love as you have walked the Camino? Hold these images in your mind. Allow them to imprint on your soul. Let them be your map for walking in love today. May the love you share be a sweet aroma to all who come across your path, and may they walk lighter because of it.

Reflections on the Day

Where did I begin today?

Where will I stay this evening?

How far have I come?

Where did beauty, kindness or generosity surprise me?

What was I thinking about or feeling?

Where did I encounter God?

Where did I most clearly see the truth of my own heart?

What is the state of my heart right now?

Other insights:

Take a few moments of prayerful silence. Use this time as an opportunity to express gratitude for the day, and ask for what you need. Trust God cares about what is on your heart and desires to meet you here.

ARRIVAL
Day Thirty-Three

It will not be long before you will take your last steps on the Camino leading to Santiago. The path will guide you through an archway, down a set of stairs and onto the Plaza del Obradoiro. Standing in the center of this massive space, the bell towers of the Cathedral of Santiago de Compostela will rise above you, stretching towards the heavens. The stairs of this great church, which lead to the Portico of Glory, will speak to your heart the words you have longed to hear, "You have arrived, come and enter."

Right now, this is only an image you hold in your imagination. Very soon, however, you will step into this picture and it will then be a glorious reality. How do you imagine it will feel to come to this important milestone on your journey? Surely excitement and joy will wash over you when you arrive. You will celebrate with those with whom you enter the city, and you will have the good pleasure of being reunited with others you met along the way. Other emotions will follow too, maybe even some sadness that the journey is now complete. Allow yourself the freedom to be present to whatever feelings come.

This freedom does not mean you cannot be intentional with what will take place. As you make your way to the cathedral ask yourself, what do I want to hold in my heart as I walk these last kilometers to Santiago? What do I desire to take away from what I am about to experience? How do I want to commemorate this momentous occasion? How will I savor this moment? Then do so.

Reflections on the Day

Where did I begin today?

Where will I stay this evening?

How far have I come?

Where did beauty, kindness or generosity surprise me?

What was I thinking about or feeling?

Where did I encounter God?

Where did I most clearly see the truth of my own heart?

What is the state of my heart right now?

Other insights:

Take a few moments of prayerful silence. Use this time as an opportunity to express gratitude for the day, and ask for what you need. Trust God cares about what is on your heart and desires to meet you here.

SILENCE
Day Thirty-Four

While it is true you had long stretches of silence as you made your way to Santiago, the silence you experience as you walk out of the city, and begin to make your way towards Finisterra, will be different. The days leading up to your arrival in Santiago were filled with anticipation and excitement. After you entered the city, you celebrated with friends, were reacquainted with people you had met along the way, engaged in the Pilgrim's Mass, lingered over dinner, and eventually said your goodbyes to many who would not be continuing on. The time was full of energy, emotion, and conversation.

Now you are leaving that all behind. It will be much quieter. Not only because there will be less people, but because you will be drawn into your own heart as you reflect on what the last few days have held. The memories created in Santiago, and indeed along the entire Camino, will be very present to you. You will long to hold on to these special moments, and the euphoric feelings you had because of them. The silence will become sacred.

In a real sense, you are walking away from what just took place. As you do, you may feel sadness. Instead of pushing these feelings aside, embrace them as testimony to the significance of your journey and the importance of the people who shared it. While you cannot hold on to the moment, you can honor it. The desire to do so may draw you further into silence. In the space it creates, be open to the movements of your heart as your body once again moves in rhythm with the Camino.

Reflections on the Day

Where did I begin today?

Where will I stay this evening?

How far have I come?

Where did beauty, kindness or generosity surprise me?

What was I thinking about or feeling?

Where did I encounter God?

Where did I most clearly see the truth of my own heart?

What is the state of my heart right now?

Other insights:

Take a few moments of prayerful silence. Use this time as an opportunity to express gratitude for the day, and ask for what you need. Trust God cares about what is on your heart and desires to meet you here.

REFLECTION
Day Thirty-Five

As you make your way to Finisterre, your mind and body is strong. You are comfortable in your pilgrim's skin, and it feels good to be back on the road. You are more comfortable with who you are and what you can accomplish. Your spirit feels lighter and free. This may become one of the most significant parts of your Camino. It is a time of recollection, reflection and looking forward. The journey to Finisterre allows life on the Camino and your life back at home to begin to be joined together.

You are still reflecting on the people you met and the experiences you shared along the way. They have become part of your story and you have been shaped by them. It is worth thinking about the transformation which has taken place. How have you grown and developed? What has this journey done to bring clarity to what you see as significant? How has it enlarged your view of the world, and your place in it? How did you grow spiritually?

You will also likely begin to think about home. You will reflect on what is most important to you, family, friends, community, faith, your vocation and the rhythm of your life. How will you integrate your expanded soul into these relationships and spaces? What are you most excited to share upon your return? What do you think will be hardest for people to understand? How do you think this journey will affect the way you relate to the most important people and roles in your life?

These reflections will help you articulate what has been most impactful to you, when you return home.

Reflections on the Day

Where did I begin today?

Where will I stay this evening?

How far have I come?

Where did beauty, kindness or generosity surprise me?

What was I thinking about or feeling?

Where did I encounter God?

Where did I most clearly see the truth of my own heart?

What is the state of my heart right now?

Other insights:

Take a few moments of prayerful silence. Use this time as an opportunity to express gratitude for the day, and ask for what you need. Trust God cares about what is on your heart and desires to meet you here.

JOY
Day Thirty-Six

There will be a moment today when you will come up over a rise and for the first time on this journey, you catch a glimpse of the sea. And joy will come. Joy is an attitude of heart and mind. It can be rooted in the anticipation of something wonderful. It can be born with the surprise appearance of an unexpected good. It is manifested in the present moment in an experience of pleasure or delight. This moment, like much of the Camino, will contain all three. Allow it to lead you to reflect back over the past month and notice the places you experienced joy.

Where on your journey did the expectation of what was to come bring you joy? Where did an unanticipated blessing surprise you with joy? What were the moments in which you experienced pleasure, delight, happiness, beauty, success, or contentment? In meditating on these things, allow the fullness of joy to wash over you. Let gladness fill your heart.

Joy is more than being happy. It is a feeling or emotion born in the confidence and hope you will see good and you will receive blessing, even if your present circumstances are hard. No doubt, you have experienced joy amidst difficult circumstances on the Camino. This has exercised and expanded your capacity for lasting joy. How does this reality invite you to turn towards home, anticipating the good which lies ahead? Can you be expectant that you will be surprised by moments of joy when you return? Is your heart prepared to be present to the blessings of your return? Carry joy home with you.

Reflections on the Day

Where did I begin today?

Where will I stay this evening?

How far have I come?

Where did beauty, kindness or generosity surprise me?

What was I thinking about or feeling?

Where did I encounter God?

Where did I most clearly see the truth of my own heart?

What is the state of my heart right now?

Other insights:

Take a few moments of prayerful silence. Use this time as an opportunity to express gratitude for the day, and ask for what you need. Trust God cares about what is on your heart and desires to meet you here.

RETURN
Home

The bus ride back from Finisterre may have been enough to open you to the reality that it is going to take time to readjust to the pace of your "normal life." You have become acclimated to walking in a different rhythm than is afforded by modern society. You have enjoyed space which has allowed you to be attuned to the world around you, your own heart and to God. You have experienced how present people can be to one another. It has all been life-giving. Watching a two-hour bus ride erase three days of walking may awaken you to the fact the transition into life back at home may be jarring to your soul. Give yourself grace. Just like you had to listen to your body to adjust to its rhythm at the beginning of the Camino, you will need to listen to your soul to understand the speed at which you can reenter.

You might want to think about how to intentionally ease back into your regular life. What disciplines of the mind, body and soul could be of aid? Continuing to journal your daily experience may help create the space you have become accustomed to. Walking will also make room for you to continue to process all that has transpired and discern how you will integrate your experience into daily life. It will also allow your body to continue to play its role in bringing you into a state of well-being. Small things like drinking a café con leche can trigger memories and feelings that help you hold on to the peace and clarity you have found in Spain. Determine what will be most helpful to you, and make it a rhythm.

Reflections on the Day

Where did I begin today?

Where will I stay this evening?

How far have I come?

Where did beauty, kindness or generosity surprise me?

What was I thinking about or feeling?

Where did I encounter God?

Where did I most clearly see the truth of my own heart?

What is the state of my heart right now?

Other insights:

Take a few moments of prayerful silence. Use this time as an opportunity to express gratitude for the day, and ask for what you need. Trust God cares about what is on your heart and desires to meet you here.

APPENDIX
Scriptures for Meditation

Numbers 6:24

> The Lord bless you and keep you;
> the Lord make his face shine on you
>   and be gracious to you;
> the Lord turn his face toward you
>   and give you peace.

Psalm 24:13 & 14

> I remain confident of this:
>   I will see the goodness of the Lord
>   in the land of the living.
> Wait for the Lord;
>   be strong and take heart
>   and wait for the Lord.

Psalm 130:5 & 6

> I wait for the Lord, my whole being waits,
>   and in his word I put my hope.
> I wait for the Lord
>   more than watchmen wait for the morning,
>   more than watchmen wait for the morning.

Psalm 131:1 & 2

> My heart is not proud, Lord,
>   my eyes are not haughty;
> I do not concern myself with great matters
>   or things too wonderful for me.
> But I have calmed and quieted myself,
>   I am like a weaned child with its mother;
>   like a weaned child I am content.

Psalm 139:23 & 24

You have searched me, Lord,
  and you know me.
You know when I sit and when I rise;
  you perceive my thoughts from afar.
You discern my going out and my lying down;
  you are familiar with all my ways.
Before a word is on my tongue
  you, Lord, know it completely.
You hem me in behind and before,
  and you lay your hand upon me.
Such knowledge is too wonderful for me,
  too lofty for me to attain.

Psalm 139:23 & 24

Search me, God, and know my heart;
  test me and know my anxious thoughts.
See if there is any offensive way in me,
  and lead me in the way everlasting.

Jeremiah 6:16

Stand at the crossroads and look;
  ask for the ancient paths,
ask where the good way is, and walk in it,
  and you will find rest for your souls.

Jeremiah 29:11

"For I know the plans I have for you," declares
the Lord, "plans to prosper you and not to harm you,
plans to give you hope and a future."

Matthew 5:3-10

Blessed are the poor in spirit,
    for theirs is the kingdom of heaven.
Blessed are those who mourn,
    for they will be comforted.
Blessed are the meek,
    for they will inherit the earth.
Blessed are those who hunger and thirst for
righteousness,
    for they will be filled.
Blessed are the merciful,
    for they will be shown mercy.
Blessed are the pure in heart,
    for they will see God.
Blessed are the peacemakers,
    for they will be called children of God.
Blessed are those who are persecuted because of
righteousness,
    for theirs is the kingdom of heaven.

Matthew 6:25 & 26

Therefore I tell you, do not worry about your life,
what you will eat or drink; or about your body, what
you will wear. Is not life more than food, and the
body more than clothes? Look at the birds of the air;
they do not sow or reap or store away in barns, and
yet your heavenly Father feeds them. Are you not
much more valuable than they?

Galatians 5:6

The only thing that counts is faith expressing itself
through love.

I Corinthians 10:13

Love is patient, love is kind. It does not envy, it does not boast, it is not proud. It does not dishonor others, it is not self-seeking, it is not easily angered, it keeps no record of wrongs. Love does not delight in evil but rejoices with the truth. It always protects, always trusts, always hopes, always perseveres. Love never fails.

Galatians 5:22 & 23

The fruit of the Spirit is love, joy, peace, forbearance, kindness, goodness, faithfulness, gentleness and self-control. Against such things there is no law.

Ephesians 3:17-19

I pray that you, being rooted and established in love, may have power, together with all the Lord's holy people, to grasp how wide and long and high and deep is the love of Christ, and to know this love that surpasses knowledge—that you may be filled to the measure of all the fullness of God.

Philippians 2:3 & 4

Do nothing out of selfish ambition or vain conceit. Rather, in humility value others above yourselves, not looking to your own interests but each of you to the interests of the others.

Philippians 4:8

Finally, brothers and sisters, whatever is true, whatever is noble, whatever is right, whatever is pure, whatever is lovely, whatever is admirable—if anything is excellent or praiseworthy—think about such things.

ABOUT THE AUTHOR

Ronald K. Ottenad is the author of the book *The Good Way, Walking an Old Road to a New Life*. It tells the story of his journey on the Camino de Santiago, which he walked in 2014. He is also a Staff Spiritual Director at the Center for Spiritual Renewal, in La Mirada, CA. He is the President of Rooted Soul Ministries, an organization which seeks to create environments where people can encounter God and learn to walk in freedom. He served as a pastor in a large church for 21 years and is currently partnering in planting a new church. He has a Bachelor of Arts Degree in Journalism from California State University, Long Beach and two master's degrees from Biola University, a Master of Arts in Organizational Leadership and a Master of Arts in Spiritual Formation and Soul Care. He has been married to his wife for 29 years and they have two children.

The end is only the beginning.
Be expectant.

Made in the USA
Coppell, TX
27 February 2025

46447289R00094